CUBA

CUBA

Grace Under Pressure

ROSEMARY SULLIVAN

PHOTOGRAPHS BY MALCOLM DAVID BATTY

INTRODUCTION BY MARGARET ATWOOD

This paperback edition published in 2004 by
McArthur & Company

First published in Canada in 2003 by
McArthur & Company
322 King St. West, Suite 402
Toronto, Ontario
M5V 1J2
www.mcarthur-co.com

Library and Archives Canada Cataloguing in Publication

Sullivan, Rosemary
        Cuba : grace under pressure / Rosemary Sullivan ; photographs by Malcolm
David Batty.

ISBN 1-55278-384-7 (bound).—ISBN 1-55278-463-0 (pbk.)

        1. Cuba. 2. Arts--Cuba. 3. Cuba--Civilization. I. Batty, Malcolm David
II. Title.

F1760.S84 2003   972.91   C2003-904014-3

Design/Composition & Cover: Tania Craan
Photographic Printing: Bob Carnie
Printed in Canada

The publisher would like to acknowledge the financial support of the Government of Canada through the Book Publishing Industry Development Program, the Canada Council, and the Ontario Arts Council for our publishing activities. We also acknowledge the Government of Ontario through the Ontario Media Development Corporation Ontario Book Initiative.

10 9 8 7 6 5 4 3 2 1

My beloved partner Malcolm David Batty passed away suddenly on August 6, 2003.
It was his wish to dedicate this book to the Cuban people.

JANE FELLOWES

To my compañero, Juan Opitz, who has opened worlds for me that I could never have travelled on my own. And to Malcolm, whom we will both deeply miss.

ROSEMARY SULLIVAN

ACKNOWLEDGEMENTS We would like to thank Bruce Westwood to whom we owe an enormous debt. He set this project in motion, and supported and nurtured it with patience and enthusiasm. It was Bruce's idea to match the elegant prose of Rosemary Sullivan with Malcolm David Batty's haunting photographs. Malcolm's first visit to Cuba in *1997* was followed by trips in *1999*, *2002*, and early *2003*. Over those six years, he took more than three thousand photographs that celebrated and captured the spirit and grace of Cuba and its people. Jane Fellowes' humour and charm kept us sane throughout. Her energy, intelligence, and confidence in this project were a constant source of strength. Juan R. Opitz was crucial to the text of this book. His vision of the historical complexity of the Latin American culture, based on lived experience, shaped our understanding of Cuba. When he said *hermanos* (brothers), Cubans believed him, and doors opened in response to his humour, integrity, and warmth. We would like to thank H.E. Carlos R. Fernández de Cossío, Cuba's Ambassador to Canada, and Rogerio Santan, Cuba's Consul General in Toronto, for their courtesy and goodwill. They always extended to us a Cuban welcome. We especially want to thank all those people in Cuba who made themselves available to us for interviews, particularly Miguel Barnet, Dulce Maria, Pablo Armando Fernández, Compay Segundo and family, Nacho and Joanna, and Ernesto and Estela Bravo for their generosity. We want to thank Agustín and Nereida Gómez for their hospitality and friendship. Thank you to Paul Knox for providing us with the names of people to contact in Cuba and for vetting the manuscript for errors; and to Graeme Gibson for his support of the project and careful reading of the manuscript. Our special gratitude goes to Margaret Atwood for taking the time out from an impossibly busy schedule to write the book's introduction. Finally, we want to thank our publisher, Kim McArthur, and the wonderful team at McArthur & Company. They had the vision to commit to this book and the determination and passion to bring it to life. We thank Tania Craan for her brilliant design, Pamela Erlichman for her precise line-edit, Tom Childs at Quadratone and the team at Friesens, and Bob Carnie, whose commitment to quality made the printing of the photographs such a pleasure for Malcolm. Our grateful thanks to all of you who made this dream a reality.

HAND ON DRUM

PANCHO QUINTO, PERCUSSIONIST

MIGUEL BARNET WITH LUPITA AND PEPETIN

LUNCH WITH MIGUEL There is always a moment when a book gels. The trepidations and anxieties of the search suddenly recede when, like a tungsten flash, a book's logic clarifies. That happened to me during lunch with Miguel.

We had arrived in Cuba the previous week in time for the opening of the National Book Fair. Many of Cuba's writers were still criss-crossing the island giving readings, and Miguel Barnet, one of Cuba's best-known poets and novelists, agreed to meet us for lunch.

We make our way to the sixteenth-century Plaza de Armas in historic Havana, threading through the park's exotic ceiba trees, their gnarled barks as textured as oil paintings, past the stalls of used books reminiscent of the bookstalls along the Seine. The booksellers shout out their wares. "You speak Spanish? French? English? What do you want? Natural history? Flora and Fauna? Ché?" When I ask for Miguel Barnet, I provoke a chain reaction. Who has Barnet? A 1967 copy of *La Sagrada*

Familia goes from hand to hand until it reaches mine. For one who loves books, it is perfect. Water-stained with a slightly musty smell, it carries the memory of forty-five years of readers.

Barnet is waiting for us at the Hotel Santa Isabel, and suggests we eat at La Tinaja on the plaza, but as we enter, a cacophony of sound sweeps over us and, daunted, we turn to leave. From a corner of my eye I catch sight of the manager leaping over the flowerbox. He does a swift turn past the fountain to head off our retreat and greets Barnet. "Sir, I have read all your work." Hastily exiling the bands of wandering musicians, he settles us in a quiet corner.

Barnet has met Batty on earlier visits and obviously likes him. Batty has the charm of an intrepid traveller. Born in India, raised in Wales, he has lived in Paris, New York, Cyprus, and Canada, and has, as he told me, driven by car on most of the world's great mountain ranges. Alert, curious, adept at finding his way into a culture, he is also rootless and seems to be searching, and perhaps part of his charm is the impression he gives that maybe you have the answer for him. However long the day and however hot, he has that mysterious British gift for still looking crisp and tidy at the end of it.

Canadian friends here for the book fair have joined us and so we are seven. I sit on one side of Barnet and Malcolm on the other. Juan sits adjacent with the tape recorder. Barnet is obviously wondering who I am and what role I will play in this encounter, for he is the centre and choreographer of the conversation. We speak in English, a language he has spoken since childhood, though his rhythms are halting and careful. "I know that man," he says of the waiter in the dark suit. He turns to him: "I have known you since childhood. What is your name?" We eat and the peacocks wandering freely through the courtyard garden approach and turn up their beaks at the proffered bread. Barnet inclines his head up and backwards, surveying the scene. There is a paradoxically slow urgency to his style. By chance we speak of painting and I ask does he know Leonora Carrington. "But she is a genius," he says in his theatrical manner. "Is she still alive?" I tell him about visiting her in Mexico. Our shoulders touch. We know now we might possibly speak a common language. It is time to look at a sample of Malcolm Batty's photographs, which he has brought with him reproduced in large format laser photocopies.

MAN DOG CAR   HAVANA

Miguel stops at a photograph of a hand. "This man is probably the grandson of a slave," he tells us. "Look at these bracelets he wears: one is probably *Changó*, the other is *Aché*. This is his past. These fingers could be the fingers of a man with a machete cutting cane in the field and being whipped in the afternoon. He is wearing a wristwatch that could have been bought in Paris or New York. This is his present. Look at his ring. Although he is thinking about his past, he also wants to show he has the right to wear a gold ring." Miguel is excited. "Generally photographers who come to Cuba never take photos of these kinds of people. They only take photos of old Havana, bloody cars, and *mulatas* with big bottoms. These photos—these are Cuba. This man is neither black nor white nor mulatto. He is Cuban."

"Ah," he enthuses, looking at the cowboys with lassos. "This rodeo is a ballet." Pausing at a photograph of a dog leaning out of the driver's seat of a car as if he were in deep conversation with a man leaning into the window, Miguel says: "This is so sweet. Look at this dog!" and remarks that a sociologist he has met is writing a book about Cubans and their dogs.

I'd been told that Miguel breeds championship Chihuahuas. "Dogs," he tells us, "at the same time as most Cubans, have entered a new period in their lives when people are loving them more. In the 1950s before the Revolution, the Public Health Department killed mongrels in the street. And now these dogs, even when they don't have good food, are kept in houses. They are loved as much as dogs with pedigrees. So dogs have also been benefited by the socialist process." He has found his passion: "Dogs have more freedom and are more democratic than we because they make love in the street whenever they want to, they eat when they are hungry." Malcolm adds an English joke: "Why do dogs lick their balls?—Because they can." "Sure," Miguel echoes, "because they can."

Next he gestures at a photograph of a child's head: "It's so sweet. His head is as polished as a globe." He looks directly at Malcolm: "I have seen many books of photographs interpreting Cuba. Other photographers come preparing a book for tourism. You have come to listen to the underground voice of Cuba, to pay tribute to the Cuban soul. We're fed up with the foreigners who wish to tell us who we are and what we should do. The Spanish still treat us like a colony. They have a saying when they lose something. 'Don't worry about losing your glasses. We lost Cuba.'

They all want to come in and take over." I think of the sign I have seen on the highway: "Lo Nuestro es Nuestro" [Ours is ours]. Self-evident, perhaps, but only to those who sit on the receiving end of power.

I say: "As a Canadian I sometimes feel like Canada is the attic to the great continental house and Latin America is the basement. One stores what one doesn't need in the attic, and buries the bodies in the basement." Miguel looks at me with warmth. "In the attic you keep your memories and in the basement you keep your treasures. The continent has lost memories and treasures." It is a more generous statement. He is suggesting we all occupy this hemisphere and are interdependent. We lose each other at a cost.

Our attention has been so totally focused that we haven't noticed the restaurant empty around us. The waiter approaches and asks Miguel for his signature. Reluctantly, we get up to leave. I now know what this book must be. I must endeavour not to interpret Cuba. This will be a journey. A journey in which I will learn a great deal.

RODEO – PARQUE LENIN

FLYING BULL   RODEO – PARQUE LENIN

MAN SLEEPING   RODEO – PARQUE LENIN

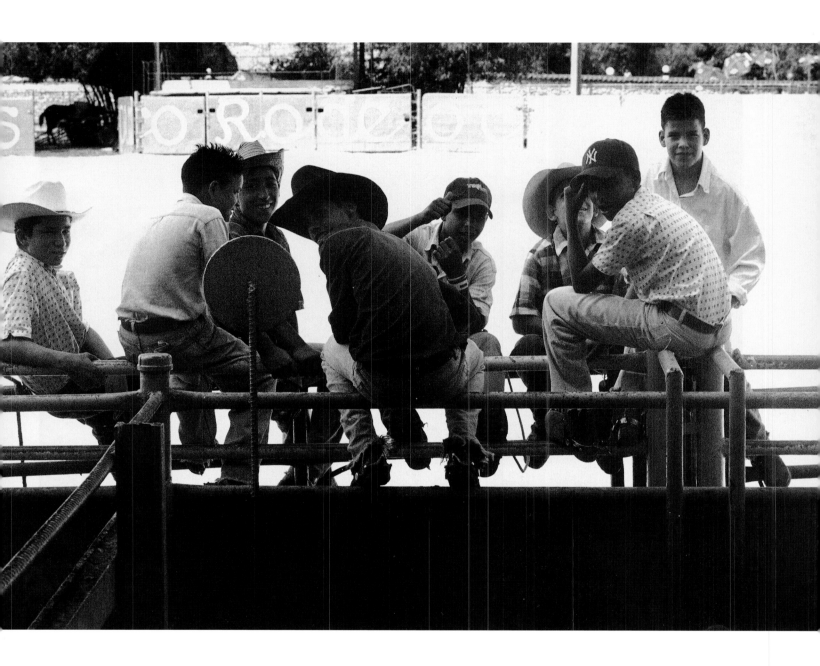

BOYS SITTING ON RAIL   RODEO – PARQUE LENIN

WEDDING   BOY WITH BRIDE AND GROOM   HAVANA

NATIONAL BALLET OF CUBA   DANCERS   HAVANA

NATIONAL BALLET OF CUBA   REHEARSAL   HAVANA

Their world was too different. But in 1959, with the Revolution, we did it again. This time we asked for a house and moved the children there and found teachers. And the government paid. At first, the children thought they were going to do athletics or judo or something, but gradually we talked about ballet and taught them. Now we have produced a generation of teachers."

"And you have produced a disproportionate number of the world's great dancers," I respond.

"Yes," she agrees. "I am very proud."

I venture a question not on my list of three: "How could you continue to dance as you lost your sight? It seems to me consummately heroic."

She is somewhat taken aback, but after a considerable silence says: "I learned to measure the stage, to feel the audience, to feel the other dancers. And before any performance I rehearsed a great deal, so that the other dancers could get used to me and know how to help me. But most of all it's inside me. I can think, I close my eyes, I can see the whole stage, I can see the whole ballet in my mind. All my life I have admired Beethoven's music, but I admire him not only as a composer but as a man because I know what it is to compose without hearing since I have had to dance without seeing."

"How do you account for Cuba's great achievement in dance, writing, painting, music?" I ask.

"I don't know," she says reflectively. "Maybe it is the mix of races, the mix of cultures that makes a wonderful combination and atmosphere. And we have been lucky to have great examples to follow, like our national poet José Martí. We have been very fortunate."

LAURA ALONSO, ALICIA ALONSO'S DAUGHTER, runs a ballet school in an unfashionable suburb of Havana. The now-derelict building was once the palace of the Countess Durañona. Underneath it can still be found a tunnel that led to the sugar mill of the adjacent plantation. In the nineteenth century, slaves used that tunnel, screening their masters from the unsightly spectacle of their trek to labour in the cane fields. The palace served as a hospital in the decade-long War of Independence in 1868. In its final incarnation, before Laura Alonso was given it for her school in 1993, it

LAURA ALONSO (RIGHT) AND FRIEND

LAURA ALONSO SCHOOL

LAURA ALONSO SCHOOL

LAURA ALONSO SCHOOL

BOY IN ANTIQUE CAR   SANTIAGO DE CUBA

EL NEGRO   HAVANA

TRAIN DRIVER   HAVANA

BLACK JESUS   SANTIAGO DE CUBA

JAZZ IN THE AFTERNOON We head by taxi to UNEAC (the Artists' and Writers' Union) for the Wednesday afternoon jazz. We vault over the sleeping policemen, as Cubans call the speed bumps here. At one stoplight all three lights—red, yellow, green—are illuminated. "Ah life, it's a choice," quips the driver. I ask about the police here. It's a *gringa* question, of course. What taxi driver the world over likes the cops? But he tells me the police are recruited from the provinces. No *Habanero* would take the job. Life's hard enough. And to impose a fine for not having the right licence, or for not having the right papers! Who but a stranger could be cruel enough to do it? "Everybody here knows everybody else," he says. A slight exaggeration, I presume, in a city of two million.

We open the wrought-iron gate, pay the admission fee of $5, and pass into the garden where table and chairs have been set among the laurel trees. Space has been cleared for a dance floor of sorts. Onstage is a group called *Danays y La Banda de la*

HERBAL REMEDIES   HAVANA

MAN SWEEPING HAVANA

FOUNTAIN IN HAVANA WITH CHILDREN RUNNING

DROPPING BY FEFÉ'S I met Fefé at a party. I was told I would be meeting the generation of young alternatives, but I don't think this applies to Fefé. Her name is Josefina de Diego and she is the daughter of one of Cuba's finest poets, Eliseo Diego. There's a skittish shyness to her that makes me think of the *zunzún*, the tiny Cuban hummingbird. Her voice is pitched low and sweet, and has a candour that is irresistible. She is anxious not to impose, and tells us to drop by anytime; she is always home taking care of her mother who is ill. I have read her story "Internal Monologue on a Corner in Havana" published in the collection *Cubana: Contemporary Fiction by Cuban Women.*

We do drop by. This is the same modest apartment her father lived in before he died in 1994. His presence is everywhere. It's as if he might return at any moment. The door opens to a book-lined living room and we are led into the small study where he wrote. Adjacent is the bedroom where her mother, who suffers from

SANTORIA WOMAN WITH CIGAR   HAVANA

ceiling above the interior stairwell reminds me of San Carolino of the Four Fountains in Rome, and the interior courtyard is tiled in Italian ceramics. We've come on time, which was a mistake. The room is too crowded to enter; we give up. Standing outside on the street, I watch a man on a motorcycle drive out of the doors of the public bus onto an elevated platform on the sidewalk. A pink bus lumbers by pulled by a diesel truck. It has two huge compartments and narrows in the middle. Cubans call these buses *camellos* [camels].

We finally slip into the concert and stand with our backs to the door. Strumming his guitar like a troubadour, Frank Delgado is singing "urban music." He's making fun of the new Cuban economy. The audience knows the lyrics by heart and is belting them out in a euphoric chorus:

I have a paladar *better than the Tocororo for you to go and eat.*
Time has passed and I've become a little impresario.
I have a licence, I pay taxes, and I have to juggle.
Don't ask me where I found the flour and the meat.

And
Ambassador of sex
Functionary of desire
During the day you study English
At night, well something else.
You don't pay taxes
If you're going to be a prostitute
At least be a proletarian prostitute.

Outside I meet Yoss. He's wearing a bandana with skull and crossbones, stud-encrusted leather wristbands and belt, and motorcycle boots. He identifies himself as a science fiction and fantasy writer published outside the country in numerous languages. I ask about his tattoos. "Realizing that tattoo artists weren't recognized in Cuba," he says, "I decided to fight for their rights and now they are officially recognized." To demonstrate their appreciation, the taboo artists gave him a free tattoo for his thirtieth birthday. He chose a Taoist symbol. He passes me his business card; his profession is *Escritor* [writer].

looking for a small group of creative people to work with. I'm learning new things and I feel pretty confident."

I can sense that Ariel is tiring and his English is beginning to fracture. I've offered to switch to Spanish, but he seems to be treating this like a challenge—will his English hold out? We chat about Frank Delgado's concert and I ask him what he thinks of Delgado? How come he gets to be critical and he isn't censored?

Ariel replies: "In Cuba they have a position for everything. If they need bottles carried they will have a position for carrying bottles: the bottle-carrying-person. I think there is a job for Delgado, for that particular person. We need some guy who doesn't say too much, who's funny, and who doesn't harm us too much. Somehow the criterion is that we can control him. OK let *him* play. And maybe there are others who won't get into it because there is already one guy sitting there. I think this happens with almost all the artists who have achieved a way to say some things."

He adds forlornly: "I've never understood why they are so concerned about it. A government that is so worried by what people might say is weak somehow. What harm can be done when people say what they feel?"

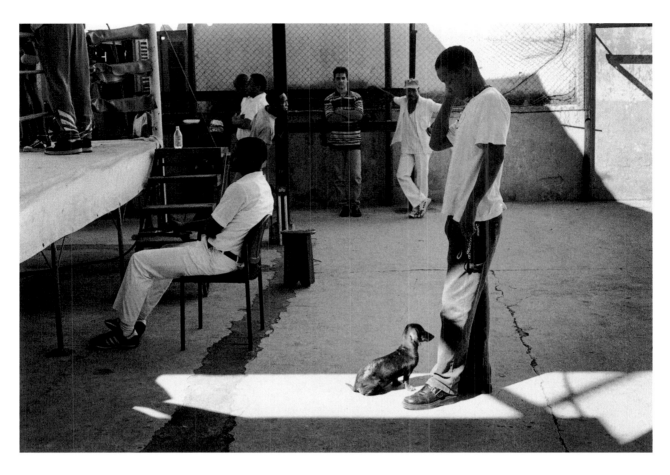

RINGSIDE   BOXEO – OLD HAVANA

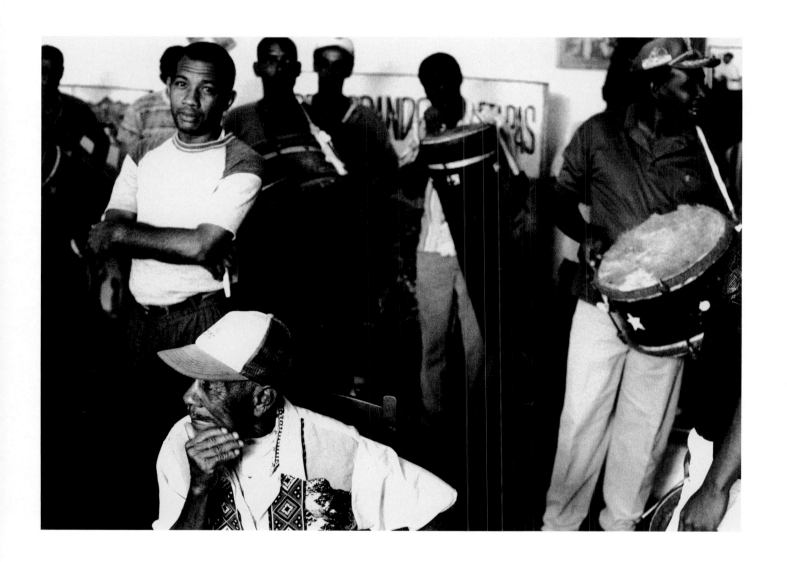

LOS OMOS   SANTIAGO DE CUBA

ERNAN LOPEZ NOSSA

BOBBY CARCASSÉS, SINGER/COMPOSER, EGREM STUDIO   HAVANA

PABLO MENÉNDEZ, MUSICIAN, AND ADRIA SANTANA, ACTOR

AT THE FOX AND CROW It's been a long day. Someone woke me at 6:30 this morning saying: "Do you have a letter [*una carta*] for me? Is this Room 619? Do you speak Spanish? What's your name?" I responded groggily: "Rosemary Sullivan. What's yours?" "Rosie," she replied. "No, I have no letter for you." She hung up. It's now 10 p.m. and we climb down the stairwell, past the bar on the left, and grab a table. About a hundred people are already crammed into *La Zorra y el Cuervo*. We could be back in the 1960s at the Village Vanguard. The room is lit with an iridescent black light that makes us look skeletal. The women's toilet is off the stage so in order to go you have to squeeze past the musicians who themselves have no dressing rooms. They hang out in the washrooms before the set. We've come to hear Pablo Menéndez. He steps onto the stage, a man in his fifties with a ponytail and broad beamed face, and tells us his group *Mezcla* is just back from a tour in the U.S. Their new disk is up for a Grammy for best Jazz CD. The black girl on the piano

149

BASS PLAYER, EGREM STUDIO   HAVANA

PAPI OVIEDO, TRES PLAYER   EGREM STUDIO   HAVANA

ERNESTO RANCAÑO, PAINTER, AT HIS STUDIO

AT THE STUDIO OF ERNESTO RANCAÑO We walk

through central Havana past a Chinatown full of colourful pagoda-roofed restaurants. The chaos and the mildly delirious din have become natural to me. I hardly notice them. This is an old idea of a city; everybody walks and the sidewalks are full of amusements. We pass the arcade where they shoot rifles; the children's playground is squeezed into a corner. The bicycle rickshaws and *colectivos* [communal taxis] crawl past the crowds. The dogs defecate on the streets. We take care to avoid the holes where the sidewalk suddenly disappears. Everywhere people are eating pizzas and pastries from the street vendors.

Ernesto lives and works above the courtyard of the same restaurant with the peacocks where we had lunch with Miguel Barnet. We climb a wooden spiral staircase gingerly because the sign says: "Careful. Staircase Under Repair," and then walk along a corridor that says: "Careful. Ceiling Under Repair," out to a roof patio that

CHILDREN PLAYING IN THE ALLEY   OLD HAVANA

BAR SILVIA   VEDADO

CANADIAN MUSICIAN JANE BUNNETT AND FRIENDS   VICTORIA BAR

VICTORIA BAR   HAVANA

THREE ON A MOTORBIKE   HAVANA

THE DEPARTURE Malcolm, who is staying on at the Vedado for another week, helps us cart our bags to the lobby. We've been here long enough to establish rituals—like our morning trips to the *Pan de Paris* for fresh croissants, which we've brought back to the hotel to eat with our *cortado* [espresso with a shot of milk]. So it feels less like leaving a hotel than leaving home. Members of the staff, Mario and Enrique and Marta, have gathered to see us off. They've ceased to be employees serving our needs, and have become persons with faces and families and private lives. We never got along with the lady at the reception, who we call the Commander since she did everything by the letter. And Mario was never quite there when you needed him; perhaps he was off watering the plants. But it wasn't about service and tips anyway. It was about talk and laughter and banter, about being easy in the tropical heat. That's Cuba.

I never remember embracing a bellhop before, but as we climb into the airport taxi, I do so now. Looking back through the window I wonder, as perhaps all

PARK   SANTIAGO DE CUBA

SIESTA BOY   HAVANA

AFTERWORD Even while we were in Cuba, the political environment was heating up. There were a number of hijackings of planes and boats. After our departure, numerous dissidents were arrested. The complexity and hardness of Cuban political life had surfaced again. But it has never been our intention to interpret Cuba or get caught up in ideological debates. The point of this book has been to let Cubans speak for themselves.

Five months after our visit to Cuba, our personal world altered irrevocably. At the end of May, Malcolm Batty was diagnosed with cancer. He died on August 6th. In my mind's eye, I will always see Malcolm striding down the Malecón, the waves leaping the seawall and breaking at his feet, young Cubans turning and shouting: "Hey, Hemingway." With his white beard and confident pace he did look like a reincarnation of Papa. If our spirits return to the places we most loved, that's where Malcolm is now, strolling down the Malecón. In his name, we dedicate this book to the patience and dignity of the Cuban people.